Laurel anc

Born in Rutherglen, Scotland, in 194
journalist and a musician. Beginning v
(1976) and *The Hardman* (1977), his popularity and reputation as a
playwright has become international. His most recent work *The
Dream Train* (written for Magnetic North Theatre Company) was read
in French translation at the Avignon Theatre Festival (2001) and
produced in Finland and in Germany. Tom McGrath now lives in
Kingskettle, Fife, Scotland, where he recently completed his latest
play, *My Old Man*.

Capercaillie Books

Laurel and Hardy

by Tom McGrath

Capercaillie Books

CAPERCAILLIE BOOKS LIMITED

First published by Midnight Press, Glasgow. Published by Capercaillie Books Limited in 2005.

Registered Office 1 Rutland Court, Edinburgh.

© 1976 Tom McGrath. The moral right of the author has been asserted.

Design by Ian Kirkwood Design.

Typeset by Chimera Creations in Cosmos and Veljovic.

Printed in Poland.

A catalogue record for this book is available from the British Library.

ISBN 0-9551246-0-3   978-0-9551246-0-0

To Ella

Characters

OLLIE: Oliver Hardy

STAN: Stan Laurel

VARIOUS VOICES

PIANIST

Act 1

OLLIE lies on stage. Behind him a screen. Shadow outline of
STAN appears on screen. The shadow figure fiddles with his
bowler. STAN crashes through the screen. Stumbles. Sits down
on top of OLLIE. Looks bemused. OLLIE wakens. Blinks. STAN
puts his hands flat on his upper legs. OLLIE lifts left hand and
puts it flat on STAN's leg. STAN tries to replace hand on his leg.
Sees OLLIE'S hand but is not clear about it. Hesitates. Puzzled.
Uses left hand to count his own right hand and OLLIE's left
hand. Indicates two with fingers of his left hand and nods his
head and smiles, well pleased with this. Then notices left hand
with which he has done the counting. Stops. Considers. Raises
right hand and counts OLLIE's left hand and his own left hand;
once again arrives at two and is well-pleased. Replaces right
hand on leg but then has problem of left hand again. Drums
fingers of left hand against his chin. OLLIE raises his left hand
from STAN's leg and counts both STAN's hands, bringing his
own hand up close to STAN's face with three fingers raised.
STAN is startled. OLLIE jumps up, sending STAN sprawling.
Woman's voice is heard on tape.

WOMAN'S VOICE: Dear ladies and gentlemen, Hal Roach presents, for
your entertainment and approval, Laurel and Hardy. We thank you . . .

OLLIE: I might have known! I thought you were going to meet me
here at 7.30.

STAN: I am.

He looks at wristwatch. Moves to exit back through screen.

OLLIE: Where are you going?

STAN: It's too early. It's only quarter to.

OLLIE: Come back. Let me look at that. **(Looks at STAN's watch.)** It's stopped.

STAN: What time is it?

OLLIE: **(consults his own watch)** It's exactly 7.30. Where have you been?

STAN: But Ollie . . .

OLLIE: Don't call me Ollie, My name is Oliver Norvell. **(He steps forward and sings to audience.)** I'm Oliver Norvell Hardy.

STAN: He's Oliver Norvell Hardy.

OLLIE: My image is big and lardy.

STAN: His image is big and lardy. He can't take a joke. He's a pompous git —

OLLIE: But full of love at the end of it.

STAN: He's always pronouncing his dignity.

OLLIE: Yes Oliver Norvell's my name.

STAN: Oliver Norvell's his name.

OLLIE: Oliver Norvell Hardy. Now there's a name, Stanley. A name destined for greatness. First the Oliver, so noble, so English. Then the Norvell – that was my beloved mother's name. And finally the Hardy, aaah . . .

STAN: Kiss me Hardy!

OLLIE: Kiss my ass! Now you stop that, Stanley. How do I look? Is my hair OK? How's about my moustache? Yoddleaeetee! My I'm in fine voice tonight.

STAN: You look like a million dollars.

OLLIE: You never saw a million dollars.

STAN: That's right. You look like nothing I ever saw. There's only one thing, Ollie.

OLLIE: And what might that be, pray?

STAN: We're dead. We've been dead for years.

OLLIE: Be quiet, fathead. Laurel and Hardy can never die!

STAN: But the people.

OLLIE: What about the people?

STAN: The people want to know who we really were.

OLLIE: They what?

STAN: They want to know who . . .

OLLIE: OK, OK, I hoid you the foist time. They want to know who we really were. They would wouldn't they? Nothing's sacred anymore. A gentleman can't have a quiet life. It was the talkies that did it.They should never have brought in the talkies. Lost all the magic. Made it too real. **(Pause)** Now what's the matter with you?

STAN: I'm scared, Ollie. Scared of telling the truth.

OLLIE: Yeah. So am I. Scared stiff.

A man's voice is heard on tape. It is the voice of James Finlayson. The boys stand frozen on the spot. STAN is crying. OLLIE has a look of dread in his eyes.

MAN'S VOICE: What do you think this is? A picnic? You're here and here you're going to stay. This is the army of forgotten souls. Men come to this Godforsaken spot to forget and be forgotten. Men come here to accept the hardships of the desert and the wastelands. To be without food and without water and to laugh at it all. Ha ha ha ha . . .

The two snap out of the freeze. OLLIE slaps STAN.

OLLIE: Now you stop that Stanley. You were always leading me astray. If it weren't for you, I'd never have landed in any trouble. You were the one. I've got absolutely nothing to hide. I shall tell the whole story. And proudly. Oliver Norvell Hardy!

They step forward and present their information to audience.

STAN: The year is 1892, Atlanta, Georgia.

OLLIE: An auspicious year in the history of man –

STAN: The year of the birth of –

OLLIE: Oliver Norvell Hardy! Yes, there I was, a beautiful child, doted on by . . .

STAN: Stop wiggling your tie.

OLLIE: What do you mean stop wiggling your tie?

STAN: Well every time you get fancy you start wiggling your tie and it just looks silly.

OLLIE: If you interrupt me again I'll wiggle you! **(Pause)** What are you crying for?

STAN: I don't want to be wiggled.

OLLIE: Oh, shut up! **(Pause)** Yes, a beautiful child doted on by one and all. My mother's name was Emily Norvell and she was of Scottish descent.

STAN: I had Scottish connections too, you know. I went to school in Glasgow although actually I was born in Lancashire in England – in Ulverston.

OLLIE: Shut up, idiot. They don't want to hear about you. I'm the one they're after, aren't I? Yes,I thought so. **(Pause)** My father has just died. My father. A lawyer. An important man in his own way – much more respectable than I ever got to be dashing about on film sets. My father, Oliver Hardy, has just died, while I am still quite young.

STAN cries.

OLLIE: Pardon me, ladies and gentleman. I wish to speak to my friend Stanley privately. **(Aside)** What are you trying to do? Ruin my speech?

STAN: No. That's impossible.

OLLIE: You bet your life it's impossible.

STAN: Ollie, that's the first time you've agreed with me.

OLLIE: Ohhh . . . Yes. It was the depression that did it.

STAN: Yea. I was so depressed I had to take pills.

OLLIE: Stanley!

STAN: Stanley was pretty depressed too!

OLLIE: **(with frustrated rage)** Ohhh . . .

STAN retreats from him and exits. OLLIE reassured now that he has gone. Resumes with audience.

OLLIE: Yes. The depression did it to us all to some extent or another. After my father died, my family went down in the world and my mother had to go out to work to feed her hungry boy.

STAN enters dressed in shawl, hat and crinoline. A tray of pies. He speaks in high Southern voice, like a woman.

STAN: Oliver Norvell! Come and get your pies!

OLLIE: Yes, Momma.

STAN stuffs pies in OLLIE's mouth. Puts baby bonnet on his head.

STAN: Why you haven't stopped eating pies ever since your father died. Come now, Oliver, sing a song for the people. He has a fine voice, you know. He always had. A boy soprano.

OLLIE: I didn't exactly stay a boy soprano all my life, mother.

STAN: Not exactly, Oliver. But you didn't change so much. You were always my little boy, even when you got to be so big. Now come on, dear and sing a song for the people. La la la . . .

STAN hums the first few bars of *Silver Threads among the Gold*. The PIANIST takes it up.

STAN: **(singing)** Darling, I am growing old . . .

OLLIE: Silver threads among the gold.

STAN: Shine upon my brow today . . .

OLLIE sneaks off stage while STAN is singing. Sudden panic from STAN as Mother.

STAN: Ma boy! Ma boy! Where's mah boy gone? Oliver Norvell! Where's he done gone? He's only eight years old.

OLLIE re-enters feigning Negro voice and moving rubber lips with his fingers to match his words as he speaks.

OLLIE: He done run away, Ma'm. Run away with the Coburn Minstrels. And he's only eight years old. He's touring all over the South and . . .

BOTH: He's only eight years old.

STAN: I wonder what's he's doing now.

OLLIE: **(on his knees, sings)** When you and I were young, Maggie . . .

OLLIE collapses into tears, bubbling into big white handkerchief. Now STAN takes the rubber lips and does the Negro voice.

STAN: What's de matter, boy?

OLLIE: I don't want to sing anymore. I just want to go back to my **(Sings)** Mammy . . .

STAN: **(as Mother)** Oliver Norvell you're home.

OLLIE: **(as OLLIE)** Take that stupid hat off!

STAN: **(as STAN)** Don't you like it, Ollie?

OLLIE: No I do not. You should wear a proper hat like me.

Puts hand to his head and realises that he is wearing baby's bonnet. Stomps on the spot with rage. STAN resumes as Mother.

STAN: My, my, Oliver! You were always so ready to be embarrassed. And you did so much want to be a footballer! Do you remember that day you ran out on to the field in your brand new outfit and the whole crowd burst into laughter?

OLLIE: That was one of the most humiliating days of my entire life.

STAN: But that was the day you learned the secret. The secret that set you up for life. You made the people laugh.

OLLIE: But ah always kept ma shoes clean.

STAN: And you made the people laugh.

OLLIE: Ah kept ma clothes impeccable.

STAN: And you made the people laugh.

OLLIE: Didn't swear in front of the ladies.

STAN: And you made the people laugh.

OLLIE: Didn't do anything like that. Didn't tell smutty jokes. Kept ma shoes clean.

STAN: Kept your ears clean. Slicked your hair. Wore pyjamas. And it was laughter, laughter, all the way.

OLLIE: On celluloid.

STAN: On celluloid. On celluloid.

A sadness to this. STAN exits. OLLIE speaks to the audience.

OLLIE: It kept the money rolling in. And there never was no reason for not being a gentleman.

OLLIE wiggles his tie and smiles, but STAN comes on carrying a large pair of stepladders which he almost lets fall on OLLIE. OLLIE catches them just in time, roaring. Piano starts up fast music. The two of them rush about stage with the ladder, trying to assemble it. The ladder closes on OLLIE's hand making him yowl with pain. He stands exasperated. Music stops. Glares at STAN.

OLLIE: It's your turn now, Stanley. Where were you born?

STAN: I don't know.

OLLIE: Fancy not knowing where you were born.

STAN: Why I was too young to remember.

STAN pushes ladder so that it starts to topple again. Music starts up. Ladder is positioned and repositioned but to no avail. Finally it seems to be in place and OLLIE attempts to step up on it but puts his foot through between the rungs. He howls with pain. Music stops. Phone rings.

STAN: Excuse me.

He lets go ladder which again almost falls on OLLIE. Goes to telephone and answers it.

STAN: Hello. **(Pause)** It sure is. **(Puts down phone. Returns to OLLIE.)**

OLLIE: Who was it?

STAN: Oh, just some fellah having a joke.

OLLIE: What did he say?

STAN: He said, 'It's a long distance from Atlanta, Georgia.' And I said, 'It sure is.'

OLLIE: Something ought to be done about these jokers.

STAN upsets the ladder. Yowl from OLLIE. Music starts up again. OLLIE takes firm hold of ladder and holds it firmly in place with both hands. Music stops. He mops his brow. Looks at STAN, exasperated.

OLLIE: Didn't you say you had an uncle?

STAN: Sure I've got an uncle. Why?

OLLIE: Now we're getting some place. Is he living?

STAN: No. He fell through a trap door and he broke his neck.

OLLIE: Was he building a house?

STAN: No. They were hanging him at the time.

He moves once more to put ladder out of balance. But OLLIE makes a sign to him to stay clear of it.

OLLIE: Go and get changed. It's your life we're after now. (**Nods his head self-righteously.**) We'll soon see how you come off.

STAN: But I don't come off, Ollie, I'm all in one piece.

OLLIE chases STAN off stage. Returns to smile at audience and make pompous business of putting on Pickard costume (top hat and cloak) and displaying card: 'A.E. Pickard, £.S.D.' He then climbs the ladder with a great deal of fuss and installs himself at the top, with the cloak wrapped around him and top hat on.

OLLIE: **(as Pickard)** The year is 1906. The place is Glasgow, Scotland. My name is Pickard and I am at the top of the ladder. A.E.Pickard – Unlimited! The richest man in town! People like to pretend that I'm a wee bit daft – and they don't like to admit that I'm around. I'm not classy enough to have so much money. So they think. You won't see my name in their fancy albums of Eminent Glaswegians, but I'm richer than the whole lot of them put together – provosts and baillies, shop-keepers and ladies – I'll be remembered when they're long forgotten. **(Pause)** One day a young stranger came to see me. I knew him immediately. **(Enter STAN in schoolboy outfit, Pickard speaks for a moment as OLLIE.)** Not yet, idiot. Get off the stage. **(Exit STAN.)** He was young Arthur Stanley Jefferson, the son of old Gunner Jefferson, the greatest showman in Scotland. He put lions out in the street to advertise his shows. He fixed his own make-up and sewed his own clothes. He could do it with the best of them up there on the stage – and he could run the Old Scotia. Why, with a father like that, that boy had greasepaint in his blood. His mother was an actress too. When I saw him there, I wondered why he'd come to me. But then I maybe wasn't the best showman in town, but I was the most successful. **(Long pause. Nothing happens.)** Stanley? . . . It's your cue, Stanley.

STAN rushes on.

STAN: How do you like me, Ollie? Sweet sixteen and never been kissed.

OLLIE: And no wonder. Now, do that again – with more dignity,

STAN exits. OLLIE wraps cloak around himself as before and climbs to the top of ladder again.

STAN: **(off)** Ready, Ollie?

OLLIE: Ready.

Enter STAN.

11

STAN: Excuse me, Mr Pickard.

OLLIE: Yes, boy?

STAN: I want to launch myself, sir.

OLLIE: You want to launch yourself in Glasgow? Are you dimwitted?

STAN: In the world, Sir.

OLLIE: Don't give me your smart talk, boy. I could buy and sell the world a thousand times. **(Pause)** As what?

STAN: What, Sir?

OLLIE: What do you want to launch yourself as?

STAN: A boy comedian.

OLLIE: A boy comedian! What an ambition! Let's have a closer look at you. **(STAN makes to climb ladder.)** Well, you've got a head-start with those hen toes and that skinny little body of yours. You've not got everything it doesn't take. What school did you go to?

STAN: I was at Rutherglen Academy, Sir, Then I went to Queen's Park School.

OLLIE: And why did you give it up? Couldn't get on with the teachers, eh?

STAN: Oh no sir. I liked the teachers and they liked me. When I played truant, I gave them free tickets for my fathers theatre so that they wouldn't tell him . . .

He has spilled the beans.

OLLIE: Aha! Your father's theatre. You let that one slip, didn't you boy? Who is your father and which theatre does he own?

STAN: My father is Arthur Jefferson. He runs the Old Scotia in Stockwell Street . . .

OLLIE: Yes, yes, we've already heard all that. **(Pause)** There can be only one reason for you to come to me, boy, only one reason: your father doesn't want you to go on the stage.

STAN: You're right, Mr Pickard. He wants me to be a manager and count the money.

OLLIE: There's worse professions than counting money, boy, especially your own money. And worst of all is pounding the boards trying to make people laugh. You take your father's advice: it won't make you famous but it'll make you decent,

STAN: But I don't want to be decent, Mr Pickard, I want to go on the stage. I just don't care about money.

OLLIE: Maybe not now when you're sixteen years old. But the time will come.

STAN: **(inspired)** I've watched them every night from the upstairs box office – their funny walks, their comical umbrellas, their jokes, their songs, the way they bend their faces, and I get this feeling – I know what they're doing – I can't put it into words but I just know what's going on with them, and I know – a boy comedian – that is what I want to be.

OLLIE: When I won't understand what a man is saying but I can see it makes sense to him, I always think, there walks an artist, a pauper but an artist. Gunner Jefferson's going to have problems if he thinks he can keep you off the stage. **(Pause)** OK. OK. I'll give you a chance. Come down to Pickard's Museum next Tuesday and you'll be launched on your incredible career.

STAN: Thank you, Mr Pickard.

OLLIE: For better or for worse.

STAN runs off happily. OLLIE descends the ladder.

OLLIE: Good evening, ladies and gentlemen, welcome to Pickard's Museum. Sorry there ain't no seats. If I put seats in, there wouldn't be room for the performers. Over there's the tattooed lady – she only costs another penny, boys, and she's worth every halfpenny of it. And there's the machines with the moving pictures. We've got a new one in this week – *How Bridget Served the Salad - Undressed*! The ladies in our three-piece orchestra are raring to go. Good evening, girls – a delight to the eye! And we've got a lot lined up for you tonight. Jugglers, singers, escapologists, dancers, snake-charmers and a Red Indian Act all the way from Bermondsey. But first on the programme tonight is a young man new to the stage. This is his very first appearance so you are all very privileged. Give him a good reception. **(Suddenly aggressive.)** Because remember, if you don't, I'll be sitting up my ladder with my box of screw nails, and I'll let you have it right in the eye. **(Happy again.)** OK, ladies and gentlemen, here he is, a new boy comedian, Arthur Stanley Jefferson.

Enter STAN as boy comedian. Top hat battered, broken umbrella, heels off shoes, tight-fitting jacket and bright check trousers.

STAN: Good evening, ladies and jellyspoons. I'm going to start tonight by singing you a little song. And you know the last time I sang this song a fellow said to me, you've got a wonderful voice, you ought to be with Carl Rosa. But Carl Rosa's dead, I said. Yes, I know, said the fellow, that's what I mean. OK. Take it away, Daphne.

PIANIST plays intro.

STAN: **(sings)** Dear Old Mother Vaudeville, she raised and taught us all. She taught us to sing and she taught us to dance, she taught us how to fall. My dad he likes plays with a serious face, I find them such a bore, when some little chitchat and a jaunty wee hat can please them so much more. A comic can kick, a comic can jump, a comic can fly through the air.

OLLIE: **(sings)** But it isn't much good it must be understood if the box office money ain't there . . .

As OLLIE sings he comes down the ladder and joins STAN. The dialogue happens to the strains of *Daisy Daisy* with the two of them dancing together.

OLLIE: You're working well, boy.

STAN: Thank you, Mr Pickard. I wonder where I'll go from here.

OLLIE: Same as all actors, I suppose. Right down the neck of a whisky bottle.

STAN: They don't all go like that. Some are successful.

OLLIE: Well, you'll need a deal more originality. You didn't use one new gag tonight. It was all something borrowed, something blue.

STAN: **(inspired)** Like a wedding! **(Music stops.)** Oh no. Is that my father out there?

OLLIE: Well, if it isn't your father it's someone damned like him. **(Music starts again.)** I wouldn't like to be in your shoes tonight, son.

STAN: Not to mention his trousers.

OLLIE: His trousers?

STAN: I told you not to mention them.

OLLIE: So those are your father's trousers you're wearing?

STAN: Well they were before I cut them down to size.

OLLIE: Dear oh dear oh dear. If I were you boy, I'd go to see him tonight and tell him the whole story. **(Sings)** The movies they came and the radio Ma Vaudeville sank without trace.

STAN: **(sings)** But Keaton and Chaplin and Babe Hardy too, had to look upon their face.

Music rises a semitone.

BOTH: **(singing)** Dear Old Mother Vaudeville. You raised and taught us all. We learned all the tricks. **(Pause. Hat exchange business.)** That we put in our flicks in your poor man's music hall.

They finish singing together and bow to audience. Black out. Clear ladder. Come back up on dim lighting. OLLIE sits upstage. He is in shirt sleeves. Wears specs. Examining figures on large sheets of paper. STAN approaches him with trepidation.

STAN: The stairs to my father's office. They've never seemed so long before. There he is, working away, just waiting to explode.

Knocks on invisible door.

OLLIE: Come in . . .

STAN enters. A long look passes between them.

OLLIE: Well come in, son. Congratulations. Would you like a whisky and soda?

They embrace. Blackout. Lights come back up to same state as for first sequence in play. The boys are once again back in Limboland. They sit, relaxing.

STAN: That was good.

OLLIE: Great fun. I liked your boy comedian.

STAN: Your Pickard was pretty good too.

OLLIE: Pretty good? It was fantastic. **(Suddenly in pain.)** My stomach hurts.

STAN: Don't think about it, Ollie. Not yet anyway.

OLLIE: But if we're going to relive the whole darned thing, we're going to have to go through all that again.

STAN: Live in the present.

OLLIE: It's kinda difficult to live in the present when you're dead.

STAN: **(sings)** Way Down Upon the Swanee River . . .

OLLIE: What are you singing that for?

STAN: Just a memory.

OLLIE: I don't recall you ever being anywhere near the Swanee River.

STAN: Well I can still sing about it, can't I? Anyway, I learned it first in the English music hall. It was my very first speaking role. Right at the start of the play there I was – sitting at the front of the stage, fishing, with my face blackened, the Brooklyn Bridge in the background and the choir singing . . . You sing it Ollie. **(OLLIE begins to sing *Swanee River*.)** I look up and I say, 'Well, I guess'n calculate, I kent ketch no fish with that tarnation mob a-singing'. Gee whiz!

OLLIE: Did you really say that?

STAN: For sure.

OLLIE: Some of the things we actors have to say. It's amazing, isn't it? What was that I said to you in that first movie we were in together? 'Put 'em up, insect . . . ' No, that's not it. Funny, I've forgotten it.

STAN: What's funny about it?

OLLIE: Well I always remembered it when I was alive.

STAN: Something's messing with our heads, Ollie.

OLLIE: I'm coming round to that very same conclusion.

STAN: You're what?

OLLIE: I'm coming round to . . . oh, never mind. We've got to do something about this . . . **(Shouts)** Hellohoh . . . Are you the-er?

STAN: **(also shouting)** Ye-es. I'm right beside you.

OLLIE: Be quiet! . . . **(Shouts)** Hello? . . . Is there anyone out there? **(Pause. No answer.)**

STAN: What does that mean, Ollie?

OLLIE: Well It either means that there is someone there but they're not . . . **(Pause)** Do you ever get the feeling that you are being watched?

STAN: **(shivers)** Do you mean there might be . . . g-ghosties?

OLLIE: Well, what else are we?

STAN points off right and screams with fright. OLLIE points off left and screams with fright. STAN screams again, pointing. OLLIE again, same business. STAN screams again and whimpers.

OLLIE: Just a minute. What were you screaming at?

STAN: Why I was screaming at what you were screaming at.

OLLIE: But I was screaming at what you were screaming at.

STAN: And what was that?

OLLIE: That's what I want to know.

STAN: Well, I'm not waiting around any longer to find out. No, sir. I'm catching the first boat out of here. **(Exits)**

OLLIE: Stanley! Come back here! Well, how do you like that? Deserts me in my hour of need! And he calls that friendship. **(Looks at audience. Smiles, ingratiatingly, but registering alarm with his eyes.)** Pardon my friend, Mr Laurel. He had to go and see a man. **(Chuckles lightly to audience as if he's sure they'll understand. Loud banging noise off. Looks apologetically at audience and smiles. Plaster falls from above. He dusts himself off and twiddles his tie at audience. But looks up in alarm as if more dust threatens to fall. Waves cutely to member of audience. More dust falls. Alarm in his face. Recovers. Blows kiss to member of audience.)** My, oh my, but you're such a cute little thing. **(More banging. More alarm. Panic in his feet. Looks at PIANIST. Smiles)** Maestro . . . **(Raises his hand for him to play. PIANIST plays introduction to *Somebody's Coming to my House*.)**

OLLIE: **(sings)** Somebody's coming to my house. Who will it be? Wait and see. Somebody's coming to my house and they're coming for me . . .

Enter STAN with suitcase bearing label, 'California here I come'. Crosses stage behind OLLIE who turns around but fails to see him. STAN exits other side. OLLIE continues with song.

OLLIE: **(sings)** She's maybe not the kind of girl you would expect in my surrounds, but soon as she's here, you will believe that she's the one I want around.

Pause. STAN crosses stage again, in opposite direction. Now he looks very weary and can hardly carry his case. Again OLLIE looks around too late to catch sight of him.

OLLIE: **(sings)** Somebody's coming to my house. Please stay with me for a while . . .

Without OLLIE seeing him, STAN moves in on piano. Crouches down behind keyboard.

OLLIE: **(sings)** For somebody's coming to my house, and when she does . . .

Pause in song which PIANIST is supposed to cover with arpeggio. What is played is extravagant to say the least. OLLIE's eyes flick nervously sideways in direction of piano but he doesn't notice it is STAN that is playing. Attempts to finish song.

OLLIE: **(sings)** And when she does . . . **(More extravagance from piano.)** You'll see me . . . **(Piano berserk. OLLIE clenches his fists.)** . . . smile! **(He smiles smarmily at audience, then scowls round at piano. Sees STAN.)** I might have known! What do you think you're up to ruining my song like that?

STAN raises his hands to reveal that he is wearing boxing gloves. OLLIE stomps on the spot and bellows. STAN comes out from behind the piano and throws a few punches in his direction. OLLIE goes and sits down in chair. STAN picks up props for his next role as Tony the barber. He wears a white jacket and carries a shaving bowl and brush. He ties a bib round OLLIE's neck.

STAN: Ah, Mr Hardy. You wanta shave?

OLLIE: Sure do, Tony. I've just got me a job with Lubin Motion Pictures. You'll be seeing a lotta me from now on.

STAN: There's a lotta you to see, Mr Hardy. Say, how much are they paying you?

OLLIE: Why d'you want to know that?

STAN: I want to know how crazy the movie business is.

OLLIE: Maybe you should get a job in movies yourself.

STAN: I dunno. Why don't you ask Tony?

OLLIE: But you are Tony.

STAN: OK, OK, ask me then.

OLLIE: OK, Tony, why don't you want to be a movie star?

STAN: Around here everybody's a movie star, I want to be something different.

Starts to shave him.

OLLIE: Back in Georgia I showed movies for three years.

STAN: Musta been a longa show.

OLLIE: Then I decided I could do just as well myself.

STAN: Aha! So you'll be the great lover, eh? Rhubarb Vaselino!

OLLIE: No, I guess with my shape I'll be playing the heavy.

STAN: Ah. Your shape it OK, Mr Hardy. You're like a nice-a big *bambino*. **(Pats his cheeks with powder.)** You got the nice-a softa baby cheeks. Nice-a Babe. Nice-a Babe.

OLLIE: Will you stop that. Tony? Because of you the boys on the location have started calling me Babe.

STAN: So whatsa wrong with that?

OLLIE: Well, my name is Oliver Norvell . . .

STAN: Oliver Normal? What kinda name is that? In your business a name's important. Look at Mussolini. He had three brothers, but they all had the wrong names. *Bene. Bene.* Nice-a Babe. Nice-a Babe.

OLLIE: Babe Hardy! I've got an awful feeling this is going to stick.

STAN: No. Tha's OK. I wash it off later.

STAN as TONY covers Babe's face in lather – all of it. OLLIE emerges from lather and blears at the audience. A slow burn. Jumps at STAN, mad again.

OLLIE: So how were you doing in the States then, Stan?

STAN: Rock bottom, Ollie. Rock bottom. Things got so bad I stole some bread.

OLLIE: You'll need to try a new line of business. **(Exits)**

STAN: I am, Ollie, I'm going to go into movies.

STAN moves upstage for dog scene. STAN has a whisky bottle from which he takes a slug. Beside him is a little toy dog on wheels. He talks to the dog.

STAN: What are you looking so long in the face about? You think you've got problems. You're lucky you're just a dog. **(Chuckles)** His Master's Voice. **(Mimics voice which used to prelude old phonograph records.)** Edison Bell. Edison Bell. **(Pause)** Yes, sir. They're all getting their voices heard far and wide these days, on the wonderful new gramophone record **(Sings)** With 'is 'ead tooked oonderneath 'is arm, he walks t' the bludy tower. With 'is 'ead tooked oonerneath 'is arm at the Midnight Hour. **(Chuckles)** Yes, sir dog. **(Toasts him.)** Here's one in yir eye – would you like a drop – sir dog. Yes and Charles Chaplin . . . **(Trails off on this, suddenly depressed.)** Charles Chaplin has signed up to make motion pictures. He's gonna be famous. While me, Stan Jefferson, his old roommate and partner – what do I get? 'The management's gone bust. We can't pay the wages'. And here I am, all alone in the United States of Harmonica, without a ticket home. Working in a shadow theatre. And drinking too much. **(Takes another slug from bottle.)** I'm telling you, dog, never be an understudy. **(Sings)** Dear Old Mother Vaudeville, I'm left out in the cold. **(Continues speaking.)** Because you know, I was able to understudy for Charlie because I came right out of the same kennel . . . if you'll pardon the expression . . . and . . . are you alright, dog? Hey, maybe you and I could go on the stage together. You and me and a lady. That would be nice, eh, dog? You could jump through hoops. Dance on your hindlegs. Play on the violin. You'd have to be good though because she'd be a fine dancing lady. Very sexy. You'd have to behave yourself. But I wouldn't. Heh heh heh. And we'd tour all the best places. Top of the bill. The Stan Jefferson Trio. You'd be the most famous dog in the country. **(Mood changes.)** Yes, that's it. I need a partner. Cumon we'll go walkies and we'll see if any nice ladies stop to pat you . . . **(Gets up and walks with the dog a bit. He puts dog off. Returns.)** And that was what happened. I did meet up with someone else. Mae Dahlberg. An Australian dancing girl. We were a wow in vaudeville together, and we fell into each other's arms. Eventually she became the bane of my life. But it was her who gave me my name.

OLLIE sits in double bed with female wig on. He has become Mae.

OLLIE: Stanley!

STAN: I've figured it out, Mae.

OLLIE: **(miming a lady)** What's that, Stan?

STAN: Why I'm so unlucky.

OLLIE: Why's that, Stan?

STAN: It's because of my name, my love, Stan Jefferson. **(Counts the letters of his name)** J . . . E . . . F . . . F . . . E . . . R . . . S . . . O . . . N.

That's nine, isn't it?

OLLIE: I think so, Stanley dear. Just a minute. **(Counting business.)** Nine is correct.

STAN: And Stan is . . . S . . . T . . . A . . . N . . . one, two, three, four . . .

OLLIE: That is correct. My you're so clever, Stanley.

STAN: And nine plus four makes . . .

OLLIE: Just a minute, Stanley, till I compute it. **(It is an enormously complex operation. They use toes, ears, noses.)** Now let's see . . . the square root of 14 multiplied by nine over three point five . . . make a suitable deduction for V.A.T. . . . if it takes four men twenty days to dig three holes there's too strong a union . . . five four three two one count-down!!! It makes thirteen, Stan dear.

STAN: Just as I thought. Thirteen letters to my name. No wonder I'm unlucky.

OLLIE: You're not so unlucky when you've got me, Stanley dear.

STAN becomes very affectionate, pulling 'Mae' close to him and caressing her. OLLIE as OLLIE objects strongly.

OLLIE: Stop that! Just get on with the story. You'll have to get another name, Stanley dearest. **(Corrects himself. Back to female voice.)** You'll have to get another name, Stanley dearest.

STAN: I heard you the first time before your voice broke.

OLLIE: **(as OLLIE)** Cut it out, wise guy, or ah'll slug yah. **(As Mae.)** Oh, I think it should be something poetic, Stanley, because you are a true poet of the comedy stage. In ancient Rome they would have given you a laurel crown.

STAN: Laurel crown? Mmm, sounds beautiful. Laurel crown. Laurel crown.

OLLIE: Stan Laurel. That's it.

STAN and OLLIE: Stan Laurel.

STAN: With a name like that I could go places.

OLLIE: We could go places, dearest.

STAN: Oh yes. We.

Looks back at Mae on the bed with trepidation. Lighting change. OLLIE gets out of the bed. Takes off wig. Puts on eyeshade. Identifies himself to audience.

OLLIE: My name's Joe Rock. Movie producer.

STAN moves straight into argumentative scene with him.

STAN: The fact is, Mr Rock, Mae and I are a team. We were together in vaudeville and we'll stay together in movies.

OLLIE: You don't say.

STAN: Where I go, she goes. That's how it is.

OLLIE: Very interesting. So whose movies you gonna be in?

STAN: Well, I've got a contract with you.

OLLIE: Without Mae Dahlberg.

STAN: Yes, but I thought that maybe, Mr Rock . . .

OLLIE: Maybe we could write a part in for her. No deal, Stan. **(Produces contract.)** You see this? This is your contract. Sure you've signed it. It's legally binding. But my name is Joe Rock and I am going to tear it up. That is how much I don't want Mae Dahlberg.

STAN: Couldn't we at least discuss the matter?

OLLIE: There's nothing to discuss. Have a look at yourself, Stan. You had to pull your jacket down when you came in the door because you've got a hole in your pants. You haven't worked for months and you've been drinking.

STAN: OK. So you don't want me. There's nothing else to say.

STAN rises to leave.

OLLIE: Where are you going, Stan Laurel? Which studio are you going to try next? Nobody wants to employ you anymore because they know that she comes with you. Sit down and think it over. If you don't do this movie, you're finished. And I'll tell you where you're going – right down the neck of a whisky bottle.

STAN: There's no need for you to speak to me like that, Mr Rock. Just because my wife and I want to continue our partnership.

OLLIE: Your wife and you! A partnership! Are you crazy? She beats you about. She's ruining your career. Everyone knows that. She thinks she's a vamp and a great comedienne. But she's neither. She ain't sexy and she definitely ain't funny.

STAN: Mr Rock . . .

OLLIE: Not Mr Rock, Stan, call me Joe like you used to do in the days when you still talked to people. I'm trying to talk to you as a friend. And as an admirer.

STAN: OK, Joe. I know what you're trying to do. And why. Mae's no good for me; I know it. But it's one thing knowing and another thing doing something about it. If you say no to her being in this movie . . .

Lights change. OLLIE becomes Mae Dahlberg.

OLLIE: Whatdoyoumean, Stan Laurel, you couldn't convince him? Why I'll scratch you little eyes out for ya'. You didn't try. Go on; admit it. You just want to get out on that set on your own with all them young shelaghs, I know what's in your dirty little mind. You get right back down there and tell Joe Rock that we do it together or there's no deal. You're underselling yourself and you're letting me be insulted. Tell him if he wants Stan Laurel, you have your terms . . .

STAN: But Mae, I've already told him that.

Lights change. OLLIE becomes Joe Rock again.

STAN: You see what I mean?

OLLIE: Bring her down to the studio, Stan.

STAN: That'll just make matters worse.

OLLIE: I'm Joe Rock, Stan. You tell her I've got something for her.

STAN: There's no point in misleading her.

OLLIE: But I have got something for her.

STAN: What?

OLLIE: Mae Dahlberg came to the States from Australia, right?

STAN: That's right,

OLLIE: Well, if she came from Australia, she can go back to Australia, right?

STAN: She might buy that. If we had any money.

OLLIE: I've already bought the ticket —

OLLIE as Rock holds up the ticket. STAN looks at him.

Amazed silence.

STAN: But Joe, I love her.

OLLIE: When I look at you, Stan, I don't see a funnyman – I see a great comedian. And I don't want to see him destroy himself.

STAN: But I love her, Joe. Don't you understand?

OLLIE: You don't love her, Stan. You're scared stiff of her.

STAN: **(thinks it over for a moment)** OK. What do you want me to do?

OLLIE: Bring her down here and let me talk to her. The very next day you'll be working in movies again. And in the evening we can have a drink, with some female company – new female company. She'll catch the first boat out of your life or my name's not Joe Rock.

Piano plays *Waltzing Matilda*. STAN and OLLIE wave hankies after the departing Mae.

STAN: **(to audience)** Mae loved me. She always loved me. Even after I was dead, in her old age she said she loved me . . .

Puts on striped jacket. OLLIE has golf bag. He takes driver out and does a swing, as if lifting ball off tee.

OLLIE: Fore!

STAN: Hal Roach, I want to talk to you **(To audience.)** Now I'm Leo McCarey. Another movie director.

OLLIE puts golf bag upon his shoulder. Walks a bit, STAN as Leo has to try to keep up with him.

OLLIE: And I'm Hal Roach. The boys were my invention! So what you want to talk about when I'm out at my golf?

Stops. Takes bag off shoulders. Considers imaginary ball.

STAN: You remember you were on about how we needed to find some answer to Harold Lloyd?

OLLIE: Mmhm. Harold's cornered the market. **(Takes out mashie.)**

STAN: Well, I've just seen the rushes for *Lucky Dog* and I've had an idea. The big fat man . . .

OLLIE: Babe Hardy.

STAN: And the little skinny man.

OLLIE: Stan Laurel.

STAN: The sight of them together gave me an idea.

OLLIE: Why not make a movie!

STAN: How did you know that?

OLLIE: That's how all your ideas begin.

STAN: Yeah put them together in a movie.

OLLIE: We just have done.

STAN: We base the whole story around them. A double act.

OLLIE: Yeah, double act. I suppose it would be cheap.

STAN: More than that. It would sell. There's a market for it.

OLLIE: Yeah and it would be cheap

STAN: It's the kind of thing that could be used in any programme.

OLLIE: Wouldn't cost too much, yeah. How did you see it working?

STAN: Well, I was thinking – Babe, there's a touch of the Southern gent to him. So we could make him that way – trying to be smooth and debonair, that's a joke for a start. But then Stan turns up and he's some kind of bumpkin relation.

OLLIE: He's from Scotland.

STAN: Yeah, well that's it, isn't it? We could have him wearing one of those Scotch skirt things –

OLLIE: A kilt.

STAN: Yeah, one of them. And the other thing is – you know Stan – the bumpkin cousin's after the dames and that causes Babe no end of embarrassment. What with the kilt, and the hairy things, it could be a riot.

OLLIE: We could make it a two-reeler. 'Stan, get your pants on. Put your pants on, Stan . . . ' We can figure it out.

STAN: If it works out we could make it a series, Hal. People would get to know their names.

OLLIE: Babe Hardy and Stan Laurel. Ollie Hardy and Laurel . . . Laurel and Hardy . . . OK. Let's give it a try.

Piano starts up with cuckoo theme. They put on bowlers and bow ties. Move forward and take up white boiler suits splashed with paint, retaining bowlers on their heads, so that now they are two guys out to do some painting and decorating. They have buckets and wallpaper. Distemper brushes, etc. They start into business of pasting up the wallpaper which leads to STAN flicking paste into OLLIE's face. OLLIE retaliates by flicking a bigger lump of paste on to STAN. Nods his head with satisfaction. But STAN picks up

piece of wallpaper and sticks it on to OLLIE. Starts to smooth it down on OLLIE's face. Rage from OLLIE behind wallpaper. STAN makes holes for eyes, nose and mouth with his fingers. Image of OLLIE standing with wallpaper on head. In fury he tears it off. Picks up brush and plasters STAN from head to toe. STAN picks up bucket of paste and places it over OLLIE's head so that it pours down him. STAN thumps the bucket, which is on OLLIE's head, with brush. Rage and dancing feet while OLLIE extricates himself from bucket. Picks up another bucket and throws the contents in STAN's direction. But that bucket is empty. OLLIE stops, exasperated.

OLLIE: Now wait a minute. Isn't this silly? Here we are, two grown-up men, acting like a coupla children. Why we ought to be ashamed of ourselves, throwing things at one another.

STAN: Well, you started it.

OLLIE: I did not.

STAN: You certainly did not.

OLLIE: Didn't.

STAN: Did.

OLLIE: Didn't.

Pause.

OLLIE: Can't we stop this quarrelling. No more arguments from now on.

STAN: No more arguments.

OLLIE: Isn't it silly? That's why we never get any place.

STAN: Where are we going, Ollie?

31

OLLIE: We're not going anywhere! And don't call me Ollie.

Pause. OLLIE realises he has lost his temper again. Attempts to control himself.

OLLIE: Let's put our brains together so as we can forge ahead. Remember. United we stand, divided we . . .

OLLIE takes a step back and slither on the mess of paste on stage. Falls. OLLIE lies on his back.

OLLIE: You had nothing else to do. So you thought you'd come around and see me. Here I was for the first time in my life having a nice peaceful time and you had to come and spoil it. **(Pause)** Well, what have you brought me anyway.

STAN: I've brought you some hardboiled eggs and nuts, Ollie.

OLLIE: You know I can't eat that. Why didn't you bring me some candy?

STAN: Well, you didn't pay me for the last lot I brought you.

OLLIE: **(disgusted)** Hardboiled eggs and nuts! Mmmmph! Another fine mess.

Puts his thumb through an egg which turns out not to be hardboiled at all. The yolk goes over him.

Act 2

Enter STAN AND OLLIE dressed in sailor suits.

STAN: The Movies. The Groovies. Oh do you know a better way of passing your time than making movies? The Ladies – Drive you Crazies – Is there anything more dangerous to do with your time than chasing ladies?

OLLIE: The golfing – Hal Roaching – Oh do you know a better way of wasting your time than going out golfing? Horse racing – Tail chasing – Oh do you know a better way of wasting your dough than betting horses?

BOTH: The funnies – Bring in the monies – Oh wasn't that a lucky way for us to make a dime By making funnies?

OLLIE: Mr Laurel.

STAN: Yes, Mr Hardy?

BOTH: Oh tell me is there anyone that you would rather be than Laurel and Hardy? Oh tell me is there anyone that you would rather be than Laurel and Hardy? Oh tell me is there anyone that you would rather be than Laurel and Hardy? Oh no there ain't.

OLLIE hits STAN. STAN kicks OLLIE. OLLIE hits again. STAN kicks again. OLLIE removes STAN's tie. STAN removes OLLIE's tie, then flicks his nose. OLLIE hits. STAN kicks, kicks and kicks again. OLLIE tears STAN's hankie. STAN removes OLLIE's hankie to his own pocket. OLLIE hits. STAN kicks and kicks again. OLLIE throws down STAN's hat. STAN throws down OLLIE's hat. OLLIE stamps on hat, picks up other hat and places it on his head. It is too small. STAN picks up crushed hat. Sees it isn't his. Takes his own hat from OLLIE's head. Smiles. OLLIE hits. STAN kicks. OLLIE looks hard at STAN's

33

waistcoat. Rips it. STAN rips OLLIE's jacket. OLLIE hits. STAN kicks. Freeze.

OLLIE: The birth.

STAN: Of sound.

BOTH: The birth of sound.

OLLIE: Andre Deed. First clown of the movies.

STAN: Sound finished him. He ended as a nightwatchman at the Pathe Studios.

OLLIE: Max Linder. He made the future of film comedy.

STAN: He and his wife died in a suicide pact.

OLLIE: The Keystone Cops.

STAN: All stark raving mad.

OLLIE: Larry Semon.

STAN: Died of worry at the age of 39. **(They get happier.)**

OLLIE: Harry Langdon.

STAN: Was completely forgotten.

OLLIE: Raymond Griffiths.

STAN: Didn't have a voice.

OLLIE: Charlie Chaplin!

STAN: He didn't speak until 1940.

OLLIE: Buster Keaton and Harold Lloyd.

They look at each other sadly.

BOTH: We won't go into that! **(They get happier.)**

OLLIE: But W.C. Fields was fulfilled by sound.

STAN: As indeed were . . .

OLLIE: Edgar Kennedy . . .

BOTH: and James Finlayson.

They both go down on one knee and raise a hand saluting Finn. Maybe his image appears on the screen. His voice is heard on the tape. 'She gave it to you to give to me but you gave it to him to give to me but he gave it to her . . . ' (etc.)
    Tape ends. STAN on his feet. OLLIE too. Now they are BABE and STAN on film set. STAN with megaphone. Both of them in sailor suits.

STAN: OK, everyone. Stand by. **(Through megaphone. Then waves his arms.)** Right Joe. **(Speaks to OLLIE.)** You got those lines, Babe? Or you want we should run them again?

OLLIE: I got 'em.

STAN: OK, girls.

He and OLLIE take in imaginary girls, who are joining them. Each offers each of them an arm.

STAN: Right Joe. Seconds from now. Remember to hold on to Babe's face at the end and action . . . Ready everyone? Take 1. Action!

OLLIE: This way, ladies. The soda fountain's over here. **(Tickles**

imaginary chin.) My, my, but you're a lovely little thing. Sweet as sherbet.

STAN: **(to other girl)** Oh yes, I always get seasick, every time we sail. But then I get landsick too. That's why I went to sea in the first place.

They perch on stools and smile at the girls. OLLIE whispers to STAN.

OLLIE: We've only got 15 cents, so when I ask you to have a drink, you refuse.

OLLIE turns ingratiatingly to the girls, pointing at each of them with his finger.

OLLIE: What would you like, girls? Soda . . . Soda . . . **(points at himself)** Soda . . . and what will you have, Stanley?

STAN: Soda.

OLLIE: **(to the girls)** Pardon me. **(To Stan aside.)** Don't you understand? We've only got 15 cents. Now when I ask you to have a drink, you refuse. **(As if to a child.)** Do you understand? Soda . . . Soda . . . Soda . . . and what will you have, Stanley?

STAN: Soda.

OLLIE: Just a minute, please. Pardon me once more. **(To Stan.)** Can't you grasp the situation? You've got to refuse.

STAN: But you keep asking me.

OLLIE: But we're only putting it on – for the girls. **(He says this very slowly, as to a backward pupil. STAN understands at last.)** Now, let's see. Soda . . . Soda . . . Soda . . . and my dear Stan, what will you have?

STAN: **(delighted he's got it right)** I don't want anything.

GIRL'S VOICE: Oh, but you must have something.

STAN: Alright, I'll have a banana split.

OLLIE: **(exploding)** Mmmmm-hm.

Blackout.

OLLIE: Yes, Stanley, those were the days. Out on the track. There was nothing quite like it. The jockeys in their bright colours and peaked caps, the horses flarin' at the nostrils and runnin' sweat. The fresh green track, the dark green hurdles. The water jumps shone brown. The whips were flailin'.

He looks uncomfortable. Hand to his stomach.

STAN: Nostalgia, Ollie, nostalgia. How much good money did you lose at the track?

OLLIE: Well, I had to do something to get my kicks. Say, but all the time I was out at the track, or playin' a round of golf with Hal Roach, you were in there working – editing the last movie, figuring out the next, going around the movie halls timing the laughter.

STAN: We just got our kicks in different ways. All that editing and script-writing, that was freedom for me. Nobody could get at me because I was working. **(Slower, more thoughtful.)** . . . apart from, now and again, Hal Roach.

OLLIE's hand to his stomach. Beginning to register definite pain. STAN again tries to distract him from this.

STAN: Anyway, what does it matter? I did twice the work and I got twice the money for it. That was fair enough.

OLLIE: **(in definite pain)** We must be gettin' close to 1940. Ah can feel it.

37

STAN: **(still trying to keep OLLIE's mind off things)** And you were so great in front of the camera, Ollie. Tha's where you really created. I used to be amazed at what you could do with the little I had given you. And the way you moved – for such a big guy – like a ballerina!

OLLIE: **(almost doubled up)** How far are we from 1940?

STAN: Don't think about that! Think about all the great movies we made. *Way out West. You're Darn Tootin. Another Fine Mess.* 1920 to 1930, 1930 to – **(Stops himself in time.)** – twenty years of comic genius! What a partnership!

Hands OLLIE a drink. He has managed to distract him from his pain to an extent.

OLLIE: **(recovering)** Do you remember that time I was going to be married and we started to do a jigsaw puzzle?

STAN: Haw! Haw! And the time we ate the two balls of wool and thought it was spaghetti.

OLLIE: 'Neither Mr Laurel nor Mr Hardy had any thoughts of doing wrong . . . '

STAN: 'As a matter of fact they had no thoughts of any kind.'

Both laughing. Slapping each other's hands.

OLLIE: 'You know, I'm not as dumb as you look.'

STAN: 'Are you sure I know what I'm doing?'

OLLIE: 'Put 'em both up, Insect, before I comb your hair with lead.'

Both in hysterics.

OLLIE: Ha. Ha. **(Pause)** I'm hungry. Oh for a slice of possum and yam.

Way down South.

STAN: Yes, sir, and some good old fish and chips, I can smell it.

OLLIE: **(disgusted)** Fish and chips!

STAN: All woik and no play makes Jack a dull boy!

OLLIE: Jack who?

STAN: What about a large juicy steak?

OLLIE: How about three large steaks. **(PIANIST becomes waiter.)** Oh *Garçon*, three great big steaks smothered in onions.

PIANIST: Yes, sir.

OLLIE: And don't forget – plenty of onions. Oh *Garçon*, I'll have a *demitasse*.

STAN: I'll have one too – in a large cup.

OLLIE: Oh *Garçon*, bring me a *Parfait*.

STAN: Put one on my steak too, *Garçon*.

OLLIE: You don't put *Parfaits* on steaks. Where were you brung up. Pass the oideuve. **(To audience.)** Pardon my friends ignorance.

STAN: Babe, we've bin' making movies for Hal Roach for how long now?

OLLIE: Must be close on ten years.

STAN: Ten years! That's right, Babe. Ten years. You know how many films that is?

OLLIE: I dunno, Stan, for certain.Thirty- odd?

STAN: Forty-four! Forty-four movies in ten years, Ollie – *Hog Wild*, *Big Business*, *Way out West* – I can even give you all the titles. Forty-four movies in ten years. That's more than four a year.

OLLIE: Well, so what? We've done alright out of it. Hal Roach hasn't exactly been mean with us.

STAN: Yeah, but we could've done much better – better financially and better as comics. For one thing Hal wouldn't have been able to tell us what we were doing next.

OLLIE: Well, I don't know, Stan. Hal's taken us into feature films.

STAN: That's exactly what I mean, Babe. Feature films are no good for us. That way we just become stooges for some singers and a love story. Hal's trying to force us off the two-reelers. He's just responding to pressures.

OLLIE: Hal knows the market, Stan, he knows it better than we do!

STAN: Babe, you know how shrewd Hal can be. I don't want to knock him – sure he's treated us well – but you keep thinking that just because he started off the same as we did, he's turned out the same way. He hasn't, Babe. People change. He's a director. He's not the same as you and me. When he looks at us, he's like a head shrink, figuring out how to handle us so that we will do our best for him.

OLLIE: What's wrong with that? He's a director, isn't he? That's his job. He's gotta get our best from us.

STAN: Yeah, but for what, Ollie? For what? OK, sure, Hal's a great guy to work with a comedy script – sure he really loves the craft – but you know as well as I do that at the end of the day there's only one thing he's got his eye on.

OLLIE: And what's that?

STAN: Box office, Babe. Box office. Dollars, dimes and cents.

OLLIE: **(shrugs)** Wasn't any difference with dear old Mother Vaudeville.

STAN: Yeah, but there's got to be a balance. It isn't all just about making money. If we keep jumping with the changes in the market, we'll lose everything that's good about us. It's irresponsible, Babe. We're like children. We've got to take matters into our own hands. What's the matter with you, don't you want to have control over your own future?

OLLIE: OK, OK. But how do we do it? Tell me, please.

STAN: I've told you it a hundred times.

OLLIE: **(wearily)** The contract.

STAN: That's it, Babe. Right first time. That mysterious document by which fortunes are sealed and genius misappropriated. The contract.That's where Hal Roach has got us beat. Because . . . you tell me, Babe. You should know it by this time.

OLLIE: He always gets us to sign separately.

STAN: That's right, Babe. And you know what would happen if we were to sign together.

OLLIE: We would take over.

STAN: Right again, Babe – oh this boy is brilliant – Laurel and Hardy would run their own show. And that would mean more money, Babe, a lot more money. And we would also have our freedom.

Pause. They are both silent for a moment. STAN is watching OLLIE to see what effect his words have had. OLLIE is thinking about it.

OLLIE: OK. So next time he asks me to sign, you want me to say no – not till we can sign together.

STAN: I wish you would say that as if you meant it. Babe.

OLLIE: What can I say, Stan? Look, I promise you, I'll give it a lot of thought – I really will.

STAN goes over to desk. Maybe puts on specs. Lights change OLLIE turns towards him.

STAN: **(as Hal Roach)** Sorry to keep you waiting, Babe. Thanks for coming.

OLLIE: Hello, Hal.

STAN: My but you're looking fit. All those movies must be good for you. Next time we're out on the course I won't have a look-in.

OLLIE: You don't do so badly, Hal.

STAN: Say, have you tried that number seven iron I sent round to you? Is it an improvement?

OLLIE: A vast improvement, Hal. I've been meanin' to let you know about it, but . . .

STAN: But I know, it's been a good season for outsiders.

OLLIE: I don't bet on outsiders. You know me, Hal. I only back a horse if I know for sure it's good.

STAN: But you need your risks, Babe.

OLLIE: Just so long as they're calculated.

Pause. BABE looks awkward again.

STAN: Better get down to business. Here's the contract. Babe. You can read it over if you like, but it hasn't changed since last year – except, of course, there's a bit more money in it for you.

OLLIE: Oh . . .

STAN: It's been ten years. Babe, ten great years. And they've been happy years for me. Babe. I hope they have been happy for you too at Hal Roach Studios.

OLLIE: They certainly have, Hal.

STAN: And long may they continue.

Both of them look at the contract. BABE obviously uncomfortable.

STAN: You know, I had the wildest idea, Babe. When Harold Lloyd was out at the studio last week, we were talking about the old times and looking at the pool out there, I said to Harold, 'The Boys have been ducked in that pool I don't know how many times. One day I think I'll call it 'Lake Laurel and Hardy' – as a memento.' How d'ya like that, Babe? Lake Laurel and Hardy.

OLLIE: It sure would be a great memento for The Boys. Lake Laurel and Hardy.

STAN: Except it's kind of early days to be thinking about mementos. We've got a lot of good movies more to go yet, Babe. I'm sure of that. **(Pause)** Say, Babe, you need a pen for that?

OLLIE: No, That's OK, Hal. I got one here.

Fumbles in his pocket. Slow fade. Next scene comes up and they have reversed roles. OLLIE now wears the specs and is on the HAL side of the desk.

STAN: I'm sorry, Hal, I'm not going to sign. I'm not going to sign until

Babe and I can sign together.

OLLIE: **(friendly)** That same old song again, Stan Laurel. You are so ungrateful.

STAN: It's not ingratitude, Hal, I want to do things for myself. Now don't tell me that you blame me for that.

OLLIE: I don't blame you for anythin' Stan. I just think you're being foolish. You seem to forget how you were when you had to manage on your own.

STAN: I was much younger then, I made some mistakes.

OLLIE: Yes, and who got you out of your mistakes – Joe Rock – a director, and who brought you together with Babe – Leo McCary. That's what directors are for – to keep you pointing in the right direction. Why left to yourselves you and Babe wouldn't have come together in a hundred years. Because you both wanted to make it as big stars on your own. You didn't have a director's objectivity. And it was a director first told Babe to start playing his role with that quaint Southern dignity of his. Not you. Not Babe. A director. Because a director was able to sit out there and look and see while you were doing it, and think about it for a while. Then look and see what you were like when you weren't acting, and think about that for a while. And then at the end of it, put two and two together and get six – big pompous Ollie always on his dignity. Little Stan Laurel always near to tears. And most of all the director could come to that because there was nothing inside him that was at stake.

STAN: You seem to forget Hal, that I am a director.

OLLIE: You're right, Stan Laurel. You are a director. You're one of the greatest comics I have ever seen. One of the best comic scriptwriters I have read. And who knows how to direct films the way Stan Laurel does? No-one this side of Chaplin. You really are your father's son. There's just one thing I haven't seen you do.

STAN: And what's that?

OLLIE: I haven't seen you run a theatre. You've never had to keep the business side up. That's one thing your old man could do that you can't do because you always had him to do it for you.

STAN: And that's why I have to try to do it myself.

OLLIE: **(sadly)** No, Stan. That's why you need a director. **(Pause. Holds up the contract.)** In any case, Babe has already signed. **(Pause.)**

STAN: What happened?

He looks at OLLIE questioningly, OLLIE turns away, confused and upset. They put chairs up on table and sit down. OLLIE pretends to be driving car. STAN has horn.

OLLIE: **(sings)** Fresh Fi-ish. **(Horn)** Caught in the ocean this morning. **(Horn)** Salmon, mackerel, swordfish and tuna. Ha Ha! Boy-oh-boy for the first time in our lives we're a success. A nice little fish business and making money.

STAN: You know, Ollie. I've been thinking.

OLLIE: What about?

STAN: I – I know how we could make a lot more money.

OLLIE: How?

STAN: Well, if – if we caught our own fish, we wouldn't have to pay for it, then whoever we sold it to, it would be clear profit.

Horn. OLLIE stops the car. Pulls on the brake.

OLLIE: Tell me that again.

STAN: Well, if you caught a fish and whoever you sold it to they wouldn't have to pay for it . . . then the profit would go to the fish . . . if eh . . . **(Horn)** if you caught a . . .

OLLIE: I know exactly what you mean. Your idea is to eliminate the middleman . . . That's a pretty smart thought. Here we are making pennies when we should be making dollars.

STAN: All we need is a coupla fishpoles.

OLLIE: A coupla fishpoles! With a million dollar idea like that? What we're going to do is to get ourselves a boat. **(Horn)** Fresh fish!

They jump down from chairs, sit on edge of table.

OLLIE: Mr Laurel was married . . .

STAN: Mr Hardy was also unhappy.

OLLIE: What is the surest way to keep a husband home?

STAN: Break both his legs.

They sit down on stage.

OLLIE: Sigh.

STAN: What's the matter?

OLLIE: I don't know.

STAN: I know.

OLLIE: What?

STAN: You're in love.

OLLIE: In what?

STAN: In love. L . . . U . . . G . . . H . . . Love.

OLLIE: Am I?

STAN: You certainly are.

OLLIE: How can you tell?

STAN: It's easy. Look at the silly, sloppy look on your face,

They stand up.

STAN: When the cat's away . . .

OLLIE: The mice start looking up telephone numbers.

STAN: There are greater misfortunes than being married.

OLLIE: Being married twice.

They sit down.

STAN: What are you getting so mushy about?

OLLIE: Well, I'm glad you asked me. I couldn't keep it from you much longer.

STAN: What?

OLLIE: Life's biggest moment. I'm going to be married.

STAN: You don't believe me!

OLLIE: Yes, I don't! believe . . . what do you mean you don't believe me. Didn't I just tell you I was going to be married?

STAN: Who to?

OLLIE: Why to a woman, of course. Did you ever hear of anybody marrying a man?

STAN: Sure.

OLLIE: Who?

STAN: My sister,

OLLIE: This is no time for levity. **(Pause)** She's the sweetest girl you ever saw. Well-read. Travelled all over the woild. Loved by everyone. And she's mine all mine. **(Chuckles)** Well, what do you think of it?

STAN: Who's levity?

OLLIE: Levity is a synonimum. You know what a synonimum is. A synonimum is a synonimum.

STAN: **(picking up telephone)** Hello?

OLLIE: What are you doing?

STAN: There's somebody knocking on the 'phone.

OLLIE: That's levity,

STAN: Hello, Mr Levity . . .

Knock. Knock.

OLLIE: Go to the door.

STAN goes to the PIANIST.

PIANIST: A letter for Mr Hardy.

STAN: Thank you, Mr Levity.

Gives letter to OLLIE.

OLLIE: It's from her.

Glasses business.

OLLIE: You read it.

STAN: My dear darling precious Oliver. **(OLLIE chuckles.)** As I sit writing this note to you with your picture in front of me, I have decided that all is over between us, for I love another. Your one-time sweetheart, Jean.

Moans from OLLIE.

STAN: What's the matter?

OLLIE: Didn't you read it?

STAN: Yeah, but I wasn't listening.

OLLIE: Give me that letter.

STAN: Wait a minute, there's some more, **(Reads)** 'B.S. It's best we never see each other again. Jeanie-Weenie'.

OLLIE: What does she mean, B.S.?

STAN: Big sucker, I guess.

OLLIE: Now I see it all. **(Pause)** You vampire. You wrecker of men's happiness. **(Tears letter.)** And I loined about women from you. **(Pause)** Come, Stanley.

STAN: Where are you going?

OLLIE: We're going where we can forget.

STAN: What do you mean we've got to forget?

OLLIE: None of your business. Come on.

Begins to haul him off but pauses. They stand as before.

STAN: Mr Hardy holds that every husband should tell his wife the whole truth.

OLLIE: Mr Laurel is crazy too. **(They sit down.)**

STAN: Isn't it wonderful to fall in love? I've fallen in love so many times.

OLLIE: I would have thought you wanted to forget that.

STAN: How could I forget it? That wonderful moment when you first see her late at night in a cafe somewhere. You are with your friends and she is with hers, but you can't keep your eyes off of each other. You are looking at her and she is looking at you . . . and . . .

OLLIE: And both of you are staring trouble right in the face.

STAN: Yeah, but even though you know that, you go right on, You've fallen in love — irresistible.

OLLIE: You call that love? Just because you get a rise for somebody you've only known ten seconds?

STAN: It's one of the great mysteries, Ollie — a Russian soprano, a Slavic Princess, a widow from Detroit — oh feminine magic, oh succulent feminine magic . . .

OLLIE: Must you?

STAN: **(in a reverie)** Magic. Magic. Magic.

OLLIE: And what do you do when the magic wears off?

STAN: I don't want to think about that. I prefer to make jokes about it.

OLLIE: **(laying it on thick)** Yeah, how many wives was it you had? Five was it? Six, seven? Or were some of them not your wives, it just looked that way?

STAN: Well, let me see now. If you don't count Mae, cos we never got married, though she sued me later as my common law wife — there was Lois in 1926, then Baby Ruth — I married her twice . . .

OLLIE: Why?

STAN: Well, somebody started saying I was a bigamist. Then there was the Russian Countess, I married her 3 times, then I remarried Baby Ruth and finally I married Ida.

OLLIE: That's 8 marriages, 4 divorces and 3 law suits — is there no end to this? At least I only had to change my mind once.

STAN: Twice.

OLLIE: Oh alright, twice.

STAN: So you did change it.

OLLIE: Yeah, so what?

STAN: What about your second wife, Myrtle?

OLLIE: Oh yes, Myrtle.

STAN: **(as Myrtle)** You know what I just heard, Oliver Norvell — that you were down in Tijuana of an Autumn day and you and your mistress Viola . . .

OLLIE: She was from the South like I was . . .

STAN: Heavy eye-lids and just half a smile – you and Viola blew 35 thousand dollars at the race track! Why that's eighteen weeks salary before taxes. Big Babe Hardy! Doesn't swear in front of the ladies. Keeps his shoes clean. Slicks his hair. Leaves his wife alone in a great big house to fester and can't even provide the sustenance to keep the roof over her head . . . Cheers Ollie!

OLLIE: Myrtle, don't!

STAN: Why don't you ask me for a divorce and be done with it?

OLLIE: Do we really need to go into all that?

STAN: **(as STAN again)** And during all that time, you were making comedy films and making everybody laugh.

OLLIE: Yes. So what? Where does that get us?

STAN: And afterwards, with your third wife, Lucille, you were happy?

OLLIE: Very happy.

STAN: I was very happy with my last wife too.

OLLIE: So?

STAN: So nothin' . . . I'm just beginning to feel kinda sad, that's all. I guess it must be 1940 coming up.

Piano music begins. They sing a melancholy song such as 'Shine on, shine on harvest moon, up in the sky . . . ' At the end of the song, they sit within their melancholy moods OLLIE suddenly becomes alert and excited.

OLLIE: Stanley! Stanley!

STAN's head comes up from his knees. He look around in the direction OLLIE is pointing. Nothing is visible.

OLLIE: Do you see her, Stanley, standing there? Look at her glistening eyes, her exquisite lashes, blond hair glowing like a sun in the night above the shimmer of a silver dress.

STAN is very interested but can't see anyone.

STAN: Who is it, Ollie?

OLLIE: Why, it's Jean Harlow, of course, you idiot. **(Smiling and cooing at invisible Jean.)** Who else could be so itsy-bitsy beautiful? **(Back to STAN.)** Get her a seat, Insect. **(To Jean)** Wouldn't you like to sit and rest your itsy-bitsy legs? Why certainly. That would be no problem. **(To STAN.)** Where's that seat?

STAN has been trying to communicate with OLLIE that there ain't no seats around. He tries to take the PIANIST's seat but the PIANIST repels him. Eventually OLLIE realises the situation and turns coyly to Jeenie-Weenie, toying and flapping with his tie as he does so. This gesture is frozen for a moment, then the scene continues.

OLLIE: Well, Jeenie-Weenie, there don't appear to be any seats.

Squats down gallantly with one knee out.

OLLIE: May I offer you my services, fair lady? No strings attached, of course. I'm not going to start anything I promise you that . . . Just for old time's sake so that we can have a chat . . . Lot of weather we've been having recently.

She sits down on his knee – we can tell from his face, his hands, the curve of his arm, the sexual thrill exploding on his face. As he speaks he pats an invisible Harlow bum.

OLLIE: Only nine more months till Christmas. Do you believe in Santa

Claus? You've heard all that before. I'm sure you have. Because you're irresistible.

He goes into a long long kiss, puckering his lips up to the invisible Jean who is sitting on his knee. STAN is confused by all this, and a little annoyed. He goes up to OLLIE and tries to pull him away.

OLLIE: Stop that! Go and find something useful to do. I am otherwise engaged. And I certainly don't want to be bothered by a low down no-gooder like you.

He punctuates this with an emphatic, self-righteous nod of his head. STAN moves away from him, despondent and pathetic. OLLIE continues.

OLLIE: How did you know to find me here, dearest? It must have been your woman's intuition. **(Cherubic smile on this.)** Oh mystery divine! Jeenie Weenie.

Gives her another big kiss.

STAN: Put her down, Ollie.

OLLIE: Do my ears deceive me?

STAN: No, but there's something else does.

OLLIE: Jealousy will get you nowhere. Now, get right out of here.

STAN: You're a fool.

OLLIE: And I suppose you're wise.

STAN: I'm wise to her, that's for sure.

OLLIE: **(to Jean)** Don't you listen to him, my little precious. Just you cover your bitsy ears.

Sudden loud sound of a smack. OLLIE's hand goes up to his face.

OLLIE: She's right. If I were half a man, I would knock your block off for what you've said,

STAN: Can you have forgotten already?

OLLIE: Forgotten what?

STAN: What women are like.

OLLIE: **(indignant)** Well, what are women like?

Tape of woman from film soundtrack haranguing him.

OLLIE: Yes, dear. No, dearest. Why certainly, dear. Anything you say.

STAN: Well?

OLLIE: Well OK. But you know how it is. We can't live without 'em. What else can I do? What would you do if you were in my place?

STAN: Ditch her!

OLLIE amazed at the thought.

STAN: Throw her over. Just the same as she threw you over so many many times. That's what you can do. And it's the only way that you're going to win – break her heart before she breaks yours.

OLLIE: Tell me that again!

STAN: Well, if you're in a ditch and you break a woman then her heart will throw you over before you win . . .

OLLIE: I know exactly what you mean. **(He jumps up, throwing**

invisible Jean on the floor.) Get offa my knee! Ollie this and Ollie that. Always going on at me! I know what you need to sort you out . . .

He draws back his foot to kick her. STAN restrains him.

OLLIE: I can see my own mother in her. And my first wife.

STAN: I can see my mother too.

OLLIE: She's all of the women we ever knew in our life.

Hissing sound.

OLLIE: What's she doing, Stanley, what's she doing?

STAN: She's getting bigger, Ollie. She's expanding,

The hissing sound gets louder. The two men are pushed away from one another. They are crushed by an invisible force at either side of the stage.

STAN: Ollie, she's enormous.

OLLIE: She's crushing me to death,

STAN: Do you think this is 1940?

OLLIE: No. It's my marriage breaking up.

STAN: My first love my second love my third love my fourth.

OLLIE: You and your Russian princess your widow from Detroit. I should have known.

STAN: We've had it, Ollie.

OLLIE: Aaaaaah!

The hissing is very loud. They are both being crushed into the stage, expressions of pain on their faces. There is a loud bang. A moment. They relax.

OLLIE: **(coming to himself)** What happened?

STAN: I think she bursted.

OLLIE: I think she did.

They both start laughing. Cuckoo song music begins.

BOTH: The boys are here! The boys are here! Bottle-a-beer. A thump on the ear! The boys are here! The boys are here! Now is the time for advancing!

Music continues under dialogue.

STAN: Heard the news. Babe?

OLLIE: What's that, Stan?

STAN: *The Music Box*. It's won us both an Oscar.

OLLIE: That's really swell. There's life in the old boys yet.

STAN: You betcha. And something else. We're finally going to take control of our own fate. It's fixed with Hal Roach. We're going to sign that contract together!

BOTH: **(to audience)** 1940!

Song continues. Enormous contract is flown in.

BOTH: The boys are back. And back to back. Quackety quack. Yackety yack. The boys are back. Upon the track. Back to take all their chances!

Music continues under dialogue.

STAN: I'm 50 next birthday. What age are you?

OLLIE: 48.

STAN: The best years are yet to come. **(Worried)** They've yet to go too.

Song continues, slow and laboured.

OLLIE: Growing old. My jaw unfolds!

STAN: My face is wrinkled Starting to crinkle,

Song now lively.

BOTH: But we'll be bold. Before we're old. We'll show 'em what we are made of.

They sign the contract with much biz. When STAN finishes signing, the song continues.

BOTH: Humpity Hump Humpity Hump. Dumpity Dump Dumpity Dump. Clumpity Clump Clumpity Clump. Thumpity Thump – A Clanger!

They fall, laughing.

STAN: We've done it, Babe. We've finally taken control.

OLLIE: That's right.

STAN: Without Hal Roach

OLLIE: Without Hal Roach.

STAN: What do you say, Babe, I cut ma dash, my big swank houses, my wild parties. I knew what a star should be – and now – 1940 – the

Lion is roaring – MGM, 20th Century Fox, RKO – the movie industry has grown up – and we've grown right up with it.

OLLIE: Without Hal Roach . . . With Hal we knew who we were talking to. With these new big companies . . . I dunno.

STAN: If you can change your wife, you can change your studio.

OLLIE: I only hope you're right.

STAN: Envelope One – the contract for the Marine Bases.

OLLIE: That's through already?

STAN: It sure is. Babe. It's going to be great to be doing some live performances again.

OLLIE: And something to help in that goddamned war.

STAN: Envelope Two. What does it contain? The contract with RKO! Things are moving fast in the 1940's.

Mood changes.

OLLIE: Without Hal Roach.

STAN: *Another Fine Mess*.

OLLIE: *You're Darn Tootin*.

STAN: Nobody bothers to consult me anymore about the films we make.

OLLIE: The big companies are too impersonal. To them we're just a coupla old hams.

STAN: Two old men in bowler hats trying to make their way in the world . . .

OLLIE: Smashing all the things they didn't own.

STAN: Always on the run from the cops.

OLLIE: Always trying to earn a quick buck.

STAN: And always making a muck of it.

OLLIE: 'Pardon me, lady. Could you spare a slice of bread for two victims of the Depression?'

STAN: 'And could you throw a slice of ham across mine?'

OLLIE: All kind of passé with a war in the world.

STAN: That's the great thing about wars. They keep everybody working.

OLLIE: And any excess labour – why it just gets killed off.

STAN: Adolf Hitler and Pearl Harbour.

OLLIE: Said Joseph Stalin: 'Give me the Movie Industry and I'll control the world'.

STAN: Laurel and Hardy are out of date. Who would ever have thought it.

OLLIE: When the war is over, there's the old movie industry again.

STAN: Alive and doing well on those distant shore romances. Johnny comes marching home to the sweet little girl next door and there she sits Ma Movie Industry raking in the dollars.

OLLIE: Pouring out the fantasies to an anxious little world.

STAN: And not giving a damn.

OLLIE: Not for its actors, nor its directors, but raking in the cash cutting a million-dollar dash. Louis B. Mayer. Sammy Cohen. Dollars their only reason.

STAN: You want a decision, Mr Laurel? Why we'll have to 'phone the New York bankers. They make the decisions now. Yesterday in Hollywood I was everybody's host. Today I'm nobody's guest. Come back, Hal Roach, all is forgiven.

OLLIE: Mr Laurel begins to show his age. He shows up wizened in front of the cameras.

STAN: Mr Hardy's jaws are beginning to sag . . .

BOTH: We won't go into that.

Pause.

OLLIE: **(mopping his brow)** 1950!

STAN: Well, Babe, the French appreciate us anyway. They want us to go over there and make a movie. Provisional title: *Atoll K*.

They start to hum *Old Man River* and pull forward two straw hampers. In the sequence which follows, the hampers are used to sit against, sit on top or, lie on, stand on, and finally, get inside.

BOTH: *Atoll K* – and the death is coming in – the system's breaking down – we're going round and round trying to make sense of a movie made in French.

STAN: I'm flat on my back – my heart's begun to crack.

OLLIE: And the Frenchies – are Frenching all around –

STAN: *Bonjour, Monsieur Tati.*

OLLIE: *Ah, bonjour, mon ami . . .*

STAN: What they all tawkin about, Ollie? Ah can't understand a word.

OLLIE: Where were you brung up?

BOTH: *Atoll K* – and the death is coming in – the system's breaking down – we're going round and round – trying to make sense of a movie made in French.

STAN: I'm flat on my back, my heart's begun to crack.

OLLIE: And the Froggies – are froggin' all around.

STAN: Ah, Fernandel. *Comment ca va?*

OLLIE: Oh, very well, I can't complain but my friend Mr Laurel is in some pain . . . we wanted to go to a party tonight but my friend Mr Laurel, isn't feeling quite right.

STAN: How long did we come to France for, Ollie?

OLLIE: Two months.

STAN: How long have we been here now?

OLLIE: Twelve.

STAN: Twelve months and a heart attack and the worst film we ever made. Nobody knows what the hell is going on. They all speak French and we speak English. They gave us floral bouquets. But nobody thought to get an interpreter. It's lousy. *Atoll K*, is lousy. Destroy all copies.

BOTH: DESTROY ALL COPIES.

OLLIE: *Detruire.*

STAN: *Detruire.*

OLLIE: Gall bladder. Heart. Liver. Appendix. Well, shake ma bones hang out ma skin to dry and the Good Laud will take me to the sweet by and by. A thought, another thought someone's put a violin between them and it's out of tune can't seem to string it can't seem to sing it – 'silver threads among the gold.'

STAN: Whereas ma boy gone? Oliver Norvell, where' he done gone?

OLLIE: He's run away, ma'am, with the Coburn minstrels.

STAN: And he' s only . . .

OLLIE: And he's only – **(He is inside hamper.)** – now I'm dying, I know it, when a big fat body like mine breaks down it's breaking down forever – no-one must know – except my friend, Mr Laurel.

STAN: Babe? Babe? Do you hear me. Babe? Do you understand what it is I'm saying? Wasn't it amazing that we two even met? You gave me a life worth living.

OLLIE: No-one must know – except my friend, Mr Laurel. No-one must know at all. No newspapers. No television. Because my job is to make people laugh.

He disappears inside the hamper. STAN closes it. He, does STAN LAUREL cry. Snaps into brisker mood.

STAN: Sure I still go on writing for Laurel and Hardy. Of course I do. Babe's been gone 8 years. But Laurel and Hardy's how I make sense of my life. It's my game. It keeps me sane. I put them all down on the cassette deck here – I do Babe's voice as well as my own. 'Why soitainly, that would be no problem.' And then I edit them, cut them about. It's my one abiding passion, apart from Ida. My beloved Ida.

OLLIE pops up from hamper.

OLLIE: Mr Laurel. Jerry Lewis to see you, Mr Laurel. Tony Hancock to see you, Mr Laurel. There's a whole long line of boy comedians waiting out there to see you . . .

STAN: Come in, come in . . .

STAN climbs into hamper, pulls top down.

OLLIE: Buster Keaton said at Stan Laurel's funeral. He said, 'Don't let anyone fool you. I wasn't the greatest. Chaplin wasn't the greatest. Stan Laurel was the greatest.'

STAN pops up.

STAN: If anyone turns up at my funeral with a long face, I'll never speak to them again.

Blackout. Tape music from films in blackout. When lights come up, the boys are standing on stage in classic STAN and OLLIE attire, looking as large as life. The hampers have gone.

OLLIE: Well, I certainly feel better after getting all that out of my system. No wonder my stomach was giving me such trouble.

STAN: It certainly is a blessed relief.

OLLIE: All that fuss. Why we were making molehills out of our mountains.

STAN: Yes, and life is not short enough.

OLLIE: Laurel and Hardy will go down in the annuals of time.

STAN: We are going to make somebody a whole lot of dough.

OLLIE: Now, now, Stanley. No bitterness. Not after all we have been through. You know, when I think of it, I can come to only one soitain conclusion.

STAN: What is that, Ollie?

OLLIE: Well, I was too fat and you were too thin.

STAN: Yes, and if there hadn't been any poor people, we wouldn't have been funny . . . and if we hadn't been funny . . . we wouldn't have made any money . . . and if we hadn't made any money, we would have been poor people.

OLLIE: Tell me that again.

STAN: Well, if all the people were rich, then there wouldn't be any money and if there wasn't any money, there wouldn't be any poor people.

OLLIE: I know exactly what you mean.

Music comes up on tape. It is the 'Commence the Dancing' music from *Way Out West*. They both hear it, notice it, begin to respond to it, start to do the dance just as in the film. They do the whole dance to make a happy ending to the Laurel and Hardy play. The gates of Paradise open to receive them.

The End

Shakespeare The Director's Cut
Volume 2: The Histories
Michael Bogdanov

In Act Two of The Director's Cut, Michael Bogdanov puts the Bardathon behind him and cuts to the chase by placing Shakespeare's history plays at the heart of the here-and-now, both as theatrical productions and as political interventions, profoundly pertinent to our present predicament. This is the four hundred year hurdle, and Bogdanov is going for gold. The sequel surpasses the original. The second cut is the deepest. Claiming Shakespeare as "our contemporary" can be a means of domesticating drama, denying history, and cultivating the amnesia of empire, by conveniently closing down the distance between the first Elizabethan reign and the second. No such complacency or complicity characterises Bogdanov's hardy enterprise. His purpose in regarding Henry and looking for Richard is to shake us out of our torpor. If September the 11th was a wake-up call for Tony Blair then he must have slept through Shakespeare. The stage direction for this book should read: *Alarum. Enter Bogdanov.*

> **Willy Maley, Professor of Renaissance Studies,**
> **Glasgow University**

Hardback ISBN: 0-9545206-8-8

Paperback ISBN: 09549625-9-1

Hardback Price: £16.99

Paperback Price: £10.99

Publication Date: 20/10/05

Pages: 176

Size: 129x198

Category: Literary Criticism

Distributor: Booksource

Web orders at www.capercailliebooks.co.uk

Blooded
Isabel Wright

Blooded is a rites of passage play about four sixteen year old girls coming to terms with the loss of childhood and its innocence. The once close bonds between the girls unravel, at times humourously and at times tragically. Wright's vivid portrayal of growing up makes compelling reading.

Blooded comes as a shattering deconstruction of just how fragile this sense of girl power can be . . . there's no denying the intensity of the writing.

The Scotsman

ISBN 0-9549625-4-0

£8.99

Available from Booksource
Tel: +44(0)8702 402 182 Fax: +44(0)141 557 0189
email: orders@booksource.net

Web orders at www.capercailliebooks.co.uk

Scottish
Arts Council

Dissent
Stephen Greenhorn

Greenhorn has penned a sharp comedy that looks at the government from a very different angle . . . Dissent does not dwell on the personalities of New Labour but focuses on the motives that drive politicians up the greasy pole. The play fires a broadside at the new generation of pragmatists whom the electoral landslide brought to power . . . What Dissent does very successfully is dramatise the process by which grassroots support is traded for influence inside the party.

The Guardian

ISBN 0-9545206-9-6

£8.99

Available from Booksource
Tel: +44(0)8702 402 182 Fax: +44(0)141 557 0189
email: orders@booksource.net

Web orders at www.capercailliebooks.co.uk

Scottish **Arts** Council

Electra
Tom McGrath

As a dramatist, Tom McGrath's great strength is to pare things down to the fewest possible words, the sparsest settings, only the most elemental action. This piece zings with more compressed meaning than many ten times its length. It resonates powerfully for all of us watching similar stories unfolding in the Middle East, Congo, Rwanda, the USA and Northern Ireland.

Bob Tait, Theatre Reviewer and Literary Critic

ISBN 0-9549625-2-4

£8.99

Available from Booksource
Tel: +44(0)8702 402 182 Fax: +44(0) 141 557 0189
email: orders@booksource.net

Web orders at www.capercailliebooks.co.uk

Scottish
Arts Council

Oedipus The Visionary
David Greig

David Greig's fine adaptation produces a clarity of narrative and a simple, resonant language that renders the epic accessible.

Robert Thomson, Herald

. . . an incisive exploration of the relationship between character and fate.

Sue Wilson, Independent

ISBN 0-9549625-1-6

£8.99

Available from Booksource
Tel: +44(0)8702 402 182 Fax: +44(0)141 557 0189
email: orders@booksource.net

Web orders at www.capercailliebooks.co.uk

Scottish **Arts** Council

Opium Eater
Andrew Dallmeyer

As De Quincey scribbles away in abject poverty, buoyed up by narcotic sustenance, desperately trying to meet deadlines for Blackwood his publisher, he is accompanied by a pickpocket and simpleton, Willy. The brilliant loquacious addict and the affably childish dimwit are drawn together by circumstance and a mutual need. The wonderful mastery of image in the author's work is reflected in the dialogue.

Robert Gore Langton

ISBN 0-9549625-3-2

£8.99

Available from Booksource
Tel: +44(0)8702 402 182 Fax: +44(0)141 557 0189
email: orders@booksource.net

Web orders at www.capercailliebooks.co.uk

Scottish **Arts** Council

The Salt Wound
Stephen Greenhorn

The Salt Wound ushers in not only the monumental sea but also an almost oppressive awareness of a close-knit fishing community with all its orthodoxies, traditions and celebrations. Greenhorn does a convincing job of taking the classical passions of Greek tragedy and transposing them to a modern setting. Everyone is right and wrong. No-one can do anything about it . . . It holds an audience gripped.

The Glasgow Herald

ISBN 09549625-0-8

£8.99

Available from Booksource
Tel: +44(0)8702 402 182 Fax: +44(0)141 557 0189
email: orders@booksource.net

Web orders at www.capercailliebooks.co.uk

Scottish
Arts Council

Other plays published by Capercaillie Books

Dr Korczak's Example by David Greig
ISBN 0-9545206-1-0

Kaahini by Maya Chowdhry
ISBN 0-9545206-4-5

King Matt by Stephen Greenhorn
ISBN 0-9545206-2-9

The Life of Stuff by Simon Donald
ISBN 0-9545206-6-1

Sunburst Finish by Andrea Gibb and Paddy Cunneen
ISBN 0-9545206-5-3

The Waltzer by Rhiannon Tise
ISBN 0-9545206-3-7

£5.99 each

Available from Booksource
Tel: +44(0)8702 402 182 Fax: +44(0)141 557 0189
email: orders@booksource.net

Web orders at www.capercailliebooks.co.uk